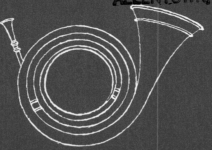

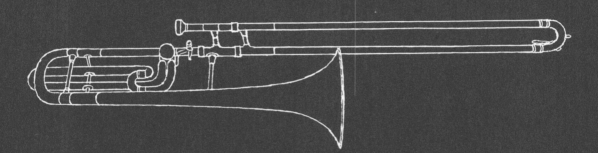

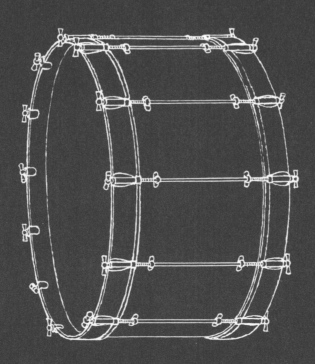

THE ORCHESTRA
AND ITS INSTRUMENTS

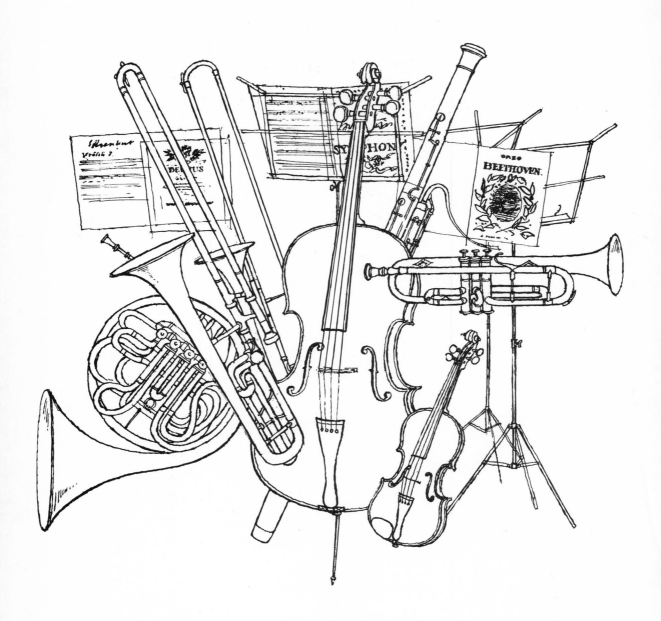

The Orchestra
and Its Instruments

CHRISTOPHER HEADINGTON

WITH DRAWINGS BY
Roy Spencer

THE WORLD PUBLISHING COMPANY

Cleveland and New York

The publishers wish to express their grateful appreciation
for permission given to reproduce photographs of members of
The National Youth Orchestra of Great Britain on pp. 11, 15, 16, 18, 19, 31, 33,
34, 44, 48, 52, 56, 57, 60, 62; p. 70 courtesy the *Sun;* courtesy *Illustrated
London News* and Sir Malcolm Sargent p. 74.
These were taken at various times by *The Daily Mirror,*
London, to whom The National Youth Orchestra has been
especially indebted for generous financial support.
The pictures on pages 26, 27, 28, 30, 42, and 46, of students
at the Interlochen Arts Academy, are reproduced by the kind
permission of the students and the Interlochen Arts Academy,
Interlochen, Michigan.

FIRST AMERICAN EDITION

Published by The World Publishing Company
2231 West 110th Street, Cleveland, Ohio 44102
Library of Congress catalog card number: 67–23357

PP

Contents

INTRODUCTION, 7

1. *The Strings,* 9

2. *The Woodwinds,* 22

3. *The Brass,* 39

4. *The Percussion,* 50

5. *Keyboard Instruments and the Voice,* 64

6. *The Conductor,* 72

7. *The Growth of the Orchestra,* 78

ORCHESTRAL EXAMPLES OF INSTRUMENTAL USE, 86

INSTRUMENTAL RANGES, 88

SUGGESTIONS FOR FURTHER READING, 91

INDEX, 93

To the members of Lancing College,
in memory of much enjoyable teaching

Introduction

For most people, there is something wonderfully exciting about the symphony orchestra. When the best part of a hundred players are working together in what could truthfully be called close harmony, when their instruments are beautiful things in themselves, and above all when the result of their cooperation can be a great musical experience—then it is not surprising that we are impressed and moved.

We should not forget that a musical experience is a shared one. The composer puts his thoughts on paper, the musicians bring them to life in terms of sound, and the listener shares in the vision which at first existed only in the composer's mind. The mystery of artistic inspiration is outside the scope of this book; so is the personal meaning of music to the music lover. But the art of playing instruments is within the reach of most people, and the enjoyment of music is within everyone's grasp. This book sets out to describe the instruments which bring us that musical enjoyment. Not every one of them is here—the guitar and the recorder are obvious omissions—but I have preferred to speak of the orchestra and orchestral instruments rather than aim at a complete catalogue. For the modern orchestra is an instrumental glory, a living tribute to man's craftsmanship and artistry—for all of us, a means to the pursuit of beauty and that consciousness of reality in its deepest sense which gives a purpose to life.

CHRISTOPHER HEADINGTON

1

The Strings

The standard symphony orchestra contains a large number of bowed string instruments: the violins, violas, violoncellos (or cellos), and double basses. It also contains one plucked string instrument: the harp. The bowed string section, which we shall call simply the string section, forms the foundation of the orchestra; the harp, on the other hand, is an instrument whose beautiful tones are usually reserved for occasional use for special effect.

The string section by far outnumbers the other members of the orchestra put together. It can contain over seventy players, with violins divided into two sections of nearly twenty each ("firsts" and "seconds"), fourteen violas, twelve cellos, and eight double basses; but for the performance of, say, a Mozart symphony, these numbers will be considerably reduced.

Unlike the woodwind, brass, and percussion groups, the string section is composed of instruments which differ from each other not in kind but only in size, and this means that there is a family resemblance of tone throughout the section. But the note middle C on a violin's G string does not sound *exactly* like the same note on a cello's A string, or on another string instrument. César Franck's fine Violin Sonata exists in a cello version: in this, most of the violin part is transposed down an octave, but the difference between the two versions is almost more striking when the cello is playing exactly the same notes. This is because of different instrumental resonances and string tensions, and the subtle variety of tone available in this way is important to a composer—just as the pleasing kinship between the instruments, which the ear recognizes, is also important.

The bowed string instruments are hollow, and each consists of a large number of separate parts—about seventy in the case of the violin. The string side is called the belly. This is normally of spruce, a soft wood, while the back and certain other parts are made of a harder wood, maple or sycamore. The fingerboard is ebony. The strings themselves are made of gut, nylon, or metal. A strip of wood, the bridge, holds them away from the belly. A violin's E string (the highest) is usually of steel; other strings often

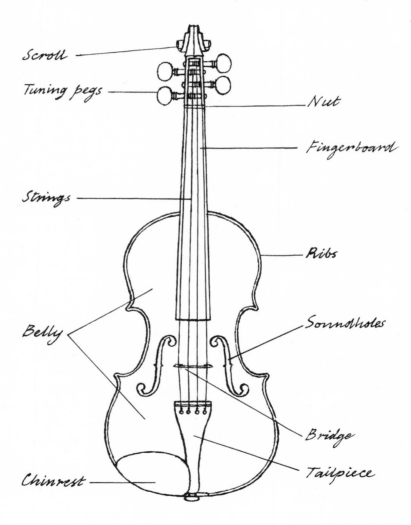

The violin

consist of a gut core wound around with metal. The bow is made of Pernambuco wood, with hair from the tails of white horses, the tension of which is slackened by a screw when the bow is out of use.

The violin, viola, cello, and double bass each have four strings, tuned as follows:

Because of its size, the double bass's strings are tuned closer together to make playing easier.

The two higher-pitched instruments are played held to the chin, while the other two stand upright. The player holds the bow with his right hand and draws it across a string. A string may be "stopped" or "open": the open string is the full length up to the bridge, but in the case of a stopped string one of the player's left-hand fingers presses the string against the fingerboard so that the vibrating length is reduced and the pitch raised. This way of pitching a note, with the bow stroke setting the string in vibration, and thus also the instrument itself and the air inside it, is the basis of bowed string technique. A vibrating movement of the finger, by very slightly varying the pitch of a note, gives an expressive quality to the sound. The left-hand thumb is not used to stop the strings, except in occasional, usually high, cello and bass passages. It is held around the fingerboard, helping to control the position of the hand and steadying the instrument. The position of the left hand is very important; it is shifted up and down the string and its positions are numbered, first position being the lowest. In the eleventh position a violinist can reach notes over two octaves higher than his highest open string.

The bow is usually drawn across a string, at right angles to it, about halfway between the fingerboard and the bridge. Playing nearer the bridge gives a glassy, hard effect (*sul ponticello*), while playing nearer the fingerboard veils the tone (*sul tasto*). These are special effects occasionally asked for by composers. A mute, a small wooden or metal clip, may be fixed over the bridge to reduce the brightness of the sound. At the direction *con sordino* a player can apply his mute in a few seconds; *senza sordino* tells him to take it off. Another effect of peculiar, ethereal beauty is that of natural and artificial harmonics, obtained by touching a string lightly with the finger at certain points along the length between the bridge and the nut (the other end of the string), or between the bridge and a normally stopped note. One of the most useful effects is that of *pizzicato*, where the string is plucked instead of bowed. In a *tremolo*, the bow is drawn rapidly backward and forward across the string.

A performer on one of the string instruments can bow on two adjacent strings simultaneously. If, at the same time, he is fingering both of them, the technique is called double stopping. By rapidly drawing the bow across the strings, changing its angle to correspond with the arch of the bridge, he can produce the effect of a chord of three or four notes. The bridge, of course, must be arched, since otherwise it would be impossible to play on either of the two middle strings without touching another.

The violin dates from around 1550. The principal violin makers of the following century and a half were Italians, the most famous being Antonio Stradivari of Cremona (1644–1737). Since that time the instrument has changed in various ways: the fingerboard has been lengthened, the string tension has been increased, the bridge has a greater arch, a chin rest has been added, and so on. But the basic design has remained the same, and many wonderful old instruments are still played today, though usually with certain

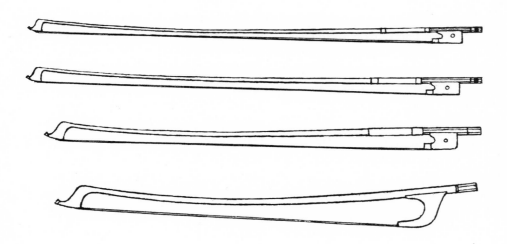

Violin, viola, cello and double bass bows, drawn to scale (reading top to bottom)

13

modifications for increased strength and brilliance of tone. The modern bow dates from about 1780, earlier bows having been shorter and more arched.

The composer Monteverdi (1567–1643) helped to establish the violin as the principal string instrument of the orchestra by featuring it prominently in his operas. As early as 1624 he used the pizzicato effect for the first time. During the period known as instrumental baroque, which lasted roughly from 1650 to 1750, the solo sonata, in which a violin was accompanied by a keyboard instrument and cello, offered possibilities for the development of violin technique, and the great school of Italian makers was matched by a distinguished series of Italian violinist-composers, of whom the most important was Corelli (1653–1713). A belated but dazzling successor to these men was Paganini (1782–1840), who carried violin technique to dizzy heights. Nowadays composers take the fullest advantage of the generally high standard of violin playing, and of an instrument with a range of nearly four octaves, throughout which a rich variety of tone is produced. But above all, violin tone, and bowed string tone in general, is the most satisfying to most listeners of all orchestral sounds.

THE VIOLA   The viola is tuned a fifth below the violin, and plays mostly in a range corresponding to the alto voice; its music is written in the alto clef, the middle line of which is middle C. In orchestral music it rarely plays much more than an octave above the highest open string, but notes up to an octave higher still can be reached. Its body length is sixteen to seventeen inches, compared with the violin's fourteen. It is as old an instrument as the violin, but was almost completely overshadowed by the more brilliant instrument until the last century. Berlioz wrote his *Harold in Italy* for Paganini in 1834 because Paganini owned a Stradivari viola which he wished to use in concert work—but in fact he never played the piece. In our own time the fine playing of the violist William Primrose has encouraged several composers to write for the viola. A number of composers have played the instrument, from Mozart to Britten and Hindemith. Hindemith, an expert performer, gave the first performance of Sir William Walton's Viola Concerto in 1929.

The viola is a mellowly beautiful instrument, less agile and bright-toned than the violin, but well suited to the expression of thoughtful, even somber music. In the orchestra and in chamber ensemble work it is indispensable, and a good amateur violist is always sure of welcome among musicians.

The violas: violins in the background

THE CELLO   The cello, or violoncello, is tuned an octave below the viola. Like the other members of the string section, it dates from the middle of the sixteenth century. It played an important part as a bass instrument in the instrumental sonatas of the baroque period, joining a keyboard instrument to form a "continuo" bass to melodic violin parts. The first cello works as such were written in 1689 by Domenico Gabrieli. Vivaldi (?1678–1741) wrote six sonatas for

Part of the cello section

cello as well as twenty concertos, and a double concerto in which the solo becomes a duet for two cellos. J. S. Bach's six unaccompanied suites are a landmark in the cello repertory; and Haydn wrote cello concertos. Since Haydn's time the instrument has been widely used and loved. It is wonderfully versatile: tender or noble in melodic playing, discreet or powerful as a bass line; and no one who has heard a good string quartet will doubt its varied beauties of tone, over a range of nearly four octaves.

The double bass has certain features in common with another family of bowed strings not used in the orchestra, the viols: its sloping shoulders and (usually) flat back, as well as its tuning in fourths. But its tone belongs nevertheless to the string section, and the features just noted are near-necessities for the player's comfort. The reason is that the instrument is very large, with a body length of 44 inches and a total length of over 6 feet. It is perhaps worth mentioning that on the rare occasions when the double bass plays in small ensembles, a smaller "chamber bass" is occasionally used. In the orchestra up to the time of Beethoven, the double basses and cellos usually shared the same part, the bass simply playing an octave lower. But for melodic use in their tenor register, the cellos had to be freed, and the basses then proved themselves quite capable of sustaining a part alone. Double bass technique is surprisingly agile for such a large instrument, and composers from Beethoven onward have not hesitated to write for it with the greatest freedom. The bass virtuoso Dragonetti (1863–1846), brought to England specially to play in Beethoven's Choral Symphony, remarked that if he had seen the music before accepting the engagement, he would have asked more than his already high fee. All the same, the bass is not often given solos in orchestral works: its tone has a rather gruff, gloomy quality, used to good effect, for example, by Mahler at the beginning of the Funeral March in his First Symphony, and—a piece of elephantine comedy —by Saint-Saëns in *Carnival of the Animals*. Harmonics and pizzicato are extremely effective. The bass, partly because of the closer tuning of the strings, has not quite the range of the other

17

The double bass

members of the string section: about three octaves, of which the top octave is rarely used. In order to reach a full octave below the cello's bottom C, some basses have a fifth string tuned to C four semitones below the normal bottom note of the instrument. Others have an extra-long fourth string: the additional length is "stopped" by a mechanical device which can, however, be released so as to make available four or even five extra semitones downward. For convenience in reading, the bass's part is written an octave higher than the true sound of the notes.

The harp is one of the most beautiful of orchestral instruments. It has a complicated ancestry, culminating in the invention, by the Frenchman Érard in 1810, of the instrument which is essentially

The harp

the one used today, the double-action harp with seven pedals. The instrument has one string to each note of the rather unusual scale of C flat major for nearly seven octaves, and one pedal corresponds to each note of the scale. The pedals may each be pushed down into two positions held by a notch: the first position raises strings by a semitone and the second by a whole tone. In this way each string can be tuned to three notes sharing the same letter name: for example, C flat, C, and C sharp. This means that the harp can play any note within its range. But chromatic writing, such as a sequence of semitones, is not really suited to the nature of the instrument, since this would call for rapid and frequent changes of pedal position. In the orchestra, the harpist is mostly asked to play chords and arpeggios, which suit it admirably. The effect called *glissando*, where the finger is drawn quickly over the strings in a sweep of sound, is often used and is unmistakable. Harmonics, delicate and ethereal in tone, are produced by touching a string at its halfway point and then plucking it with another finger, giving the note an octave higher than the written one. This effect is indicated in the player's part by a little circle above the note. A good example of harmonics and glissando together occurs in the Interlude from Britten's *A Ceremony of Carols*. Another special effect, giving a metallic sound, is that of plucking the string close to the soundboard (*près de la table*).

On the whole, composers have not used the harp a great deal for melody playing, perhaps because it cannot sustain notes very long; but Stravinsky uses it melodically to beautiful effect in the slow movement of his Symphony in Three Movements. The instrument *can* produce sounds far removed from the gorgeous splashes of color which one normally associates with it, and such as one hears in Ravel's *Daphnis et Chloé*. Britten, who seems to have a special fondness for it, has written not only conventionally lovely passages, but also others of nerve-jangling power—particularly in his opera *The Turn of the Screw*. Perhaps these are less in the character of the instrument, but one feels it has possibilities still to be explored by composers. In the meantime, the harp usually stands alone in the orchestra—although very occasionally composers require two—and is used sparingly to add its unique sound to the texture of the music.

One other member of the plucked string family which occasionally appears in the orchestra is the mandolin. This is related to the lute family and has four unison pairs of strings tuned like a violin. It is plucked with a plectrum, a small oval of tortoiseshell or similar material, and its characteristic sound is produced by a rapid thrumming of the plectrum back and forth across a pair of strings, although it can also play single notes, of course. Vivaldi, Handel, Mozart and Beethoven have used the mandolin; and in the twentieth century Mahler, Schönberg, and Stravinsky have written for it. But its tone is small and so it can only be heard in a delicate orchestral texture.

Neapolitan mandolin

2

The Woodwinds

The history of woodwind instruments takes us back to biblical times and even earlier. But the present-day orchestral instruments are relatively modern, dating from the seventeenth and eighteenth centuries. In descending order of pitch, the principal ones are flutes, oboes, clarinets, and bassoons. In addition there is the piccolo, a smaller version of the flute often met with from Beethoven's time onward, and larger versions of the oboe, clarinet, and bassoon: the English horn, bass clarinet, and double bassoon. These, too, are common in nineteenth- and twentieth-century orchestral music.

The score of Beethoven's First Symphony (1800) shows us the woodwind section in its standard form: a pair each of flutes, oboes, clarinets, and bassoons. These eight instruments do not blend in the same way as the strings do, and it takes a skillful composer to write for the whole section together without making the listener uncomfortably aware of the marked differences in tone between, say, oboe and clarinet. In the orchestra, the woodwinds are used first as soloists, holding a melodic line alone; secondly, as doubling for a tune played by, say, the strings; and lastly in full orchestral passages. Together, their range of pitch is more than five octaves— seven if we include double bassoon and piccolo. This, with their wide variety of tone color, allows them to contribute an enormous amount to the orchestra, in a classical symphony or concerto just as much as in a colorful modern work.

In these instruments, the main acoustical principle is the same: the air column inside is made to vibrate by the player's breath, and the speed of the vibration determines the pitch of the note produced. Of course if one simply blows through a tube one does not get a note at all; to produce a musical sound, the air column must be excited into vibration by one of two methods. The first, used by the flute family, is by directing the breath across an edge, and so setting up patterns of eddies inside the instrument. The second is by making a vibrating reed do the same work, as with the oboes, bassoons, and clarinets. If one blows through pursed lips, they vibrate and produce a note; a reed acts in the same way, transferring its vibrations to the air inside the instrument. With any woodwind instrument, the way in which the player blows is probably the most important part of his technique.

The other feature the woodwinds have in common is the arrangement of holes and keys down their side. The present elaborate metal systems of keywork were added gradually over quite a long period. In Bach's time, when they were fairly rudimentary, it was a good deal more difficult to play the instruments well. The holes affect pitch according to how much of the air column is enclosed and thus able to vibrate as a whole; the keys are used to close or

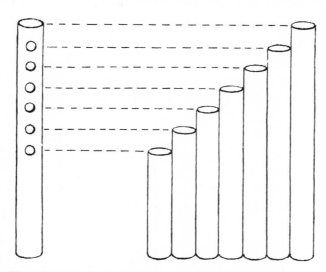

How holes in a pipe reduce its working length:
the shorter the vibrating air column, the higher the note

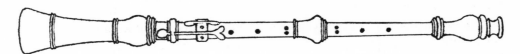

Oboe of the late eighteenth century, without its reed.
It has only two finger keys

open holes which could not comfortably be reached with a finger. But the player can get many more notes from his instrument than there are holes in its side. For one thing, it is possible to change the pitch of a note by closing a hole beyond an open one—this is called cross-fingering. For another, the harmonic series is used: the air column can be made to vibrate in two or three equal parts, giving a note an octave or a twelfth above the normal one. This technique is called overblowing.

The shape of woodwind instruments is important. The factor which makes the difference is not whether a tube is straight or bent, but whether it remains the same width all along its length. The cylindrical tubes, which do this, are the flute (apart from its "head" where the mouth hole is) and the clarinet. The oboe and bassoon are conical tubes opening out slightly toward the open end, or bell.

From left to right: oboe reed, bassoon reed, clarinet mouthpiece, clarinet reed. The final drawing shows the clarinet reed fixed into the mouthpiece

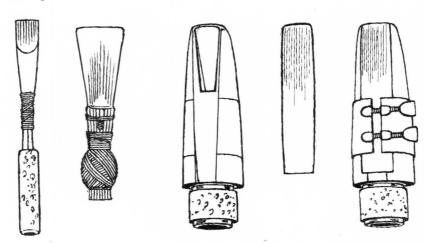

Woodwind players (except, of course, for flutists) depend greatly on their reeds. The reed is a carefully prepared and seasoned strip of what is usually called cane—it actually comes from a tall grass which grows in Southern Europe. The clarinetist has a single reed which vibrates against a slot in the mouthpiece of his instrument; oboists and bassoonists have a double reed, the two halves of which vibrate against each other and thus form the actual mouthpieces of their instruments. Reeds are delicate things and easily put out of action; woodwind players take great care of them and many like to make their own before fitting them to the instrument. They are of course interchangeable, for their working life may be quite short, sometimes only a matter of weeks.

The flute has a long ancestry, dating back much further than the Middle Ages, when the name was first commonly used. The earliest examples were cylindrical in shape; later on, about 1680, the instrument was made conical with a cylindrical mouthpiece. Still later Theobald Boehm, a nineteenth-century Munich flute player, restored the cylindrical shape, but made a slightly curved mouthpiece. He also devised a system of finger keys, so that the holes could be cut in the right places and yet remain within easy reach. The now-famous Boehm system is standard for the modern flute. The flute's range is exactly three octaves upward from middle C—after his first octave the player overblows, getting the notes one octave higher; for the third and highest octave he uses cross-fingerings.

Flutes were at one time made of boxwood, then of cocuswood. Nowadays they are usually metal—often of silver, though there have been gold flutes, and even a platinum one. This highly glamorous instrument, which belonged to the French player Georges Barrère, had a special piece written for it, called "Density 21.5" after the density of platinum!

In the orchestra the flute's nimbleness and versatility are very valuable, and it probably has more to play than any other instrument except the strings. The flutist's ability to "play anything" is well known, and so is the story of one who saw a notice in

25

The flute

Chinese and said, "I can't read it, but I think I could play it if I had my flute." The instrument has an unusually pure tone: like a treble voice, it has a clear brilliance in high passages and a wonderfully mysterious quality in low ones. Listen, for example, to the opening of Debussy's *Prélude à l'après-midi d'un faune*, or to *La Flûte enchantée* in Ravel's *Shéhérazade*. Quite a different piece, with a wide range of writing, is Bach's Suite in B Minor for flute and strings.

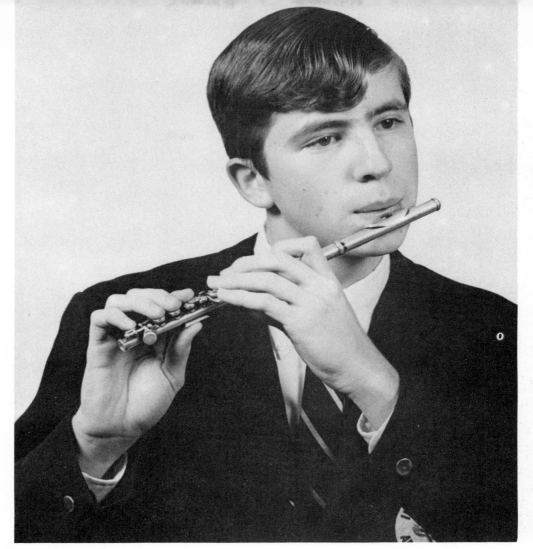

The piccolo

The piccolo is a small brother of the flute, and its history is less well known, though conical eighteenth-century examples exist. Boehm-system piccolos are conical, unlike the Boehm flute, to lessen their shrillness—for the piccolo is the highest of all orchestral instruments. It has a bright, clear tone and a range of nearly three octaves (see p. 88). Apart from its conical construction, the instrument is simply a miniature flute. Its music is written an octave lower than it actually sounds, to save the reading, and writing,

27

The oboe

of too many ledger lines. It is rarely used as a solo instrument, for its lower notes are weak, and the others are so outside the human vocal range—where even instrumental melodies are almost always written—that it has a slightly comic effect when played alone. A good example of this is the piccolo and tuba duet in the Scherzo of Britten's Violin Concerto. This is made funnier still by the extremely low tuba notes.

THE OBOE   Around 1660 the oboe replaced its forerunner, the shawm, as the standard treble reed instrument. It is conical, and played with a double reed. The oboe's tone color, once heard, is unmistakable. It has been called "the poignant, plangent oboe," but this hardly does justice to one of the most expressive instrumental sounds. It has a range of about two and a half octaves, although players can go one or two semitones higher than the top note shown on p. 89. But the extreme high notes are difficult to get satisfactorily and are little used.

Because oboes were common in the eighteenth century, and also had a stronger tone than flutes, Bach and Handel constantly used them to double violin parts in orchestral works. The oboe was one of Handel's favorite instruments, and he wrote concertos for it; by the time of Haydn and Mozart it was already well established in the orchestra. In our own time the skill and artistry of Leon Goossens have encouraged several composers to write important solo works.

The English horn is an alto oboe.* This would be a more appropriate name for it, for, as someone has said, it is neither a horn nor English. Being a deeper instrument than the oboe, it is of course longer; and it has a globular bell. Because of its length it cannot be held away from the player's body, as the oboe is, and its reed is fitted to a slim metal tube, or crook, which bends back toward the player's lips. The English horn has a range of about two and a half octaves, like the oboe, but pitched lower. Its tone is beautiful but rather melancholy. Orchestral examples of its use are common from the nineteenth century onward; two famous passages are in the slow movement of Dvorak's "New World" Symphony and Sibelius's *The Swan of Tuonela*. "In expressing ideas of sorrow and regret the instrument seems to have almost more personality than any other in the orchestra."**

The clarinet was invented by J. C. Denner, a Nuremberg maker who lived from 1655 to 1707—the date of invention is thought to be about the beginning of the eighteenth century. Its forerunner was called the chalumeau. This word is French for a reed (nowadays

THE ENGLISH HORN

THE CLARINET

* Some authorities prefer the term tenor oboe.
** Cecil Forsyth: *Orchestration.*

more often a drinking straw) and is still used to refer to the lower register of the modern clarinet. The instrument is cylindrical in shape and has a single reed. Like the oboe, it overblows with the aid of a key called the speaker key, as well as a change in embouchure—the way in which the lips are used. Because of its

The English horn

shape, the clarinet does not overblow at the octave higher, as other wind instruments do, but at the twelfth—an octave plus a perfect fifth. Mozart, in 1778, heard the pair of clarinets in the famous Mannheim orchestra and wrote to his father: "Oh, if only *we* had clarinets; you can't guess the lordly effect of a symphony

The clarinet

with flutes, oboes and clarinets." In his "Paris" Symphony, in the same year, he used a pair of clarinets himself. For Anton Stadler, a Viennese player, Mozart wrote two works which are pinnacles in the range of clarinet music, a quintet with strings and a concerto.

The tone of the clarinet is velvet-smooth and slightly hollow, especially in the low register. Two versions are used, one in B flat and the other in A (see p. 89 for ranges). A composer chooses which of these two to write for according to the key of the music—in flat keys it is normally the B flat, in sharp keys the A. This brings us to a complex but important point, that of the transposing instruments, of which the clarinet is an example. To avoid the great difficulty to the player of having to remember two fingerings for every note, according to which instrument he is playing, the notes are written so that the same fingering is used on both instruments. The note *written* as middle C is played exactly the same on the B flat and the A clarinets; but on the B flat instrument it will *sound* B flat, and on the other it will sound A. So when the composer wants middle C, he has to write another note above it: D or E flat. We have already met another transposing instrument in this chapter, the English horn, whose notes are written a fifth above the actual sound: for example G for C. This apparently complicated system actually makes playing much simpler, and a clarinetist is expected to possess both instruments—the B flat and A clarinets—and perform equally well on them. One final point about the clarinet: it is the instrument often chosen when someone takes up a woodwind instrument for the first time; it is easier to play than the others, to a moderate standard, as well as usually being cheaper to buy.

THE BASS CLARINET The bass clarinet is shaped rather like a saxophone, but is of wood, with a metal top joint and bell. In fact, it was the inventor of the saxophone, Adolphe Sax, who designed the present-day bass clarinet in 1838. It is pitched an octave below the clarinet, and is usually in B flat. Its notes are written in the treble clef an octave and a tone above their real pitch—so a clarinetist can use his

Clarinets: the bass clarinet is being played. In the foreground, the E Flat clarinet, with the B Flat and A instruments behind. The "barrel" and mouthpiece are interchangeable between the two latter instruments. The A and E Flat clarinets are shown with metal caps, which are used to protect their mouthpieces when not in use

normal treble fingering when playing the bass instrument (see p. 89 for range). There are not many bass clarinet solos, but Tchaikovsky uses the instrument prominently in the "Dance of the Sugar-plum Fairy," and Stravinsky features it in the scene in

The bassoon

the Moor's room in *Petrouchka*. Its tone varies from serpentine smoothness to an oily gurgle, and it has even been called a "bass goblin." However, it has a smoother sound in low-pitched passages than the bassoon, and provides a good bass to woodwind chords.

THE BASSOON   The bassoon has a basic design dating from the sixteenth century. To produce its low notes it needs a tube of considerable length; to make it playable, the tube is bent back on itself at the bottom joint and some of the finger holes are drilled through the wood at an angle, coming out quite a long way from where they started. Though the tube is conical, it has a narrower taper than the oboe's; and the double reed, too, is unlike that of the smaller instrument. Bassoon tone is mellow and smooth—it blends well with the horns, which oboe tone does not do. In the tenor range it comes into its own as a melodic instrument. The range is over three octaves (see p. 89), though the very top notes are difficult to play. The low register is used at the beginning of Tchaikovsky's *Symphonie pathétique*, giving a feeling of deep sadness; a famous comic dry-staccato solo is in Dukas's *Sorcerer's Apprentice;* and the opening of Stravinsky's *Le Sacre du printemps* is a beautiful and unique example of the highest range.

The double bassoon, or contrabassoon, makes an occasional appearance in the orchestra. It plays an octave lower than the bassoon (see p. 89 for its effective working range). Like the double bass's, its part is written an octave higher for easier reading. Beethoven uses it in the "Choral" Symphony, and Brahms in his First Symphony. Two good examples of double bassoon solos are by Ravel: the opening of the Piano Concerto for Left Hand, and in *Mother Goose*, "Beauty and the Beast"—there is no need to say which of these two characters is represented by the double bassoon! THE DOUBLE BASSOON

Other wind instruments make an appearance from time to time in the symphony orchestra. They include the beautiful bass flute, really an alto, which is pitched a fourth below a normal flute. There is more to it than the extra five semitones downward: it has a sleepy, antique tone quality all of its own. Stravinsky, Ravel, and Holst have used it, and so has Britten, especially in his chamber operas. There is a wonderful bass flute and bass clarinet duet in Act II of *The Turn of the Screw*, in the music preceding the scene called "The Bedroom." A bass oboe, properly speaking a baritone, is used by Holst in *The Planets*. The heckelphone also belongs to the oboe family, though it has a very pronounced conical bore. It has about the same pitch as the bass oboe, and was invented by Heckel in 1904—Strauss was the first composer to write OTHER WIND
INSTRUMENTS

35

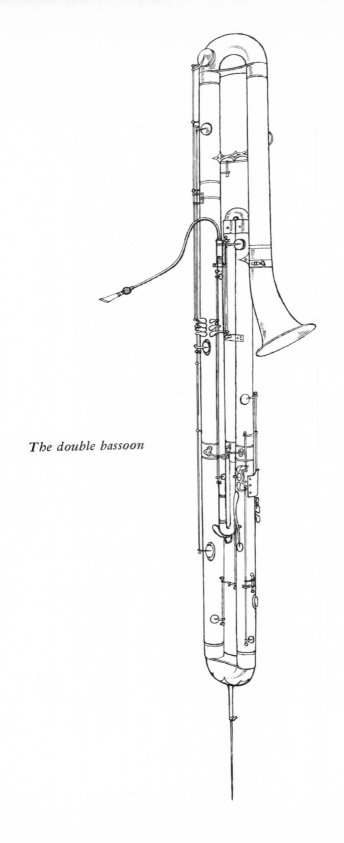

The double bassoon

for it orchestrally, in his opera *Salome*. The oboe d'amore was a favorite instrument of Bach and can be seen with its relatives in the oboe family at a performance of the St. Matthew Passion; it is pitched slightly higher than the English horn, and has a similarly shaped bell. Its tone is more veiled than that of the oboe. Military bands often have small clarinets in D and E flat, and they sometimes appear in the orchestra. In Strauss's *Till Eulenspiegel*, the D clarinet has to play one passage which uses its whole range, at the point where the hero is executed.

The saxophone belongs to a different family altogether. It is a

Soprano, alto, and tenor saxophones

single-reed instrument, like a clarinet, but its conical bore is like the oboe's, and it is made of metal. The alto, the most often used of the family, has a smooth, round tone (see p. 89 for range). The family of saxophones was invented by Adolphe Sax in the middle of the last century. Berlioz liked them, but in spite of their wide use in popular music they have never found a regular place in the symphony orchestra, although Ravel and Vaughan Williams are among those composers who have used them.

3

The Brass

The instruments of the brass section are among the noblest and most powerful in the symphony orchestra. They are the trumpets, horns, trombones, and tuba. In a full modern orchestra there are normally four horns, two trumpets, three trombones, and a tuba.

The brass instruments are relatively simple in design. The air inside a metal tube is made to vibrate as the player blows through his compressed lips. The speed of vibration of the lips affects the speed of vibration of the air column and, therefore, the pitch of the note. But it is essential to remember that just as the length of a violin string helps to determine which note it will produce, so the length of tube in a brass instrument has one fundamental note. One cannot raise this note gradually by increasing the speed of the lip vibrations, but one can change it completely by causing the air column to vibrate in sections: halves for an octave higher, thirds for an octave and four notes above, quarters for two octaves and so on. The principle is the same as in the woodwinds' overblowing and the strings' harmonics. There are two technical terms associated with this process, and we have used them both already. They are "fundamental"—the basic note of a given length of string, air or other material; and "harmonic"—one of the notes associated with the fundamental in accordance with what is called the harmonic series. The fundamental and the first four harmonics form a major chord, which may be why that chord sounds so right to our ears.

It is obvious that there are severe limitations on what a brass player can play, unless he has a way of changing the basic length of his instrument. By early in the seventeenth century, "crooks" were used on trumpets. These were interchangeable curved sections of tube of different lengths. Fitting a different crook on an instrument changed its total length, and allowed it to play a different harmonic series; but it could still play only one harmonic series until the crook was changed again. In about the middle of the eighteenth century it was found that the pitch of the horn changed slightly when the player put his hand into the bell, and this gave the horn at least more flexibility. But in about 1815— quite late in the history of the orchestra—the modern valve system was developed. This provides for an extra length of tube to be built into a brass instrument, which can be brought in by the valves, semitone by semitone, to lower the fundamental by six semitones in all—thus filling the gap between the harmonics. The trombonist solves the problem in a different way: by pushing his U-shaped slide outward he can lengthen his tube.

THE HORN   The horn derives its name from the early instruments which were actually made from the horns of animals. The hunting horns of the late Middle Ages were curved into a circular form for convenience, and it is from these that the modern instrument has developed. The horn nowadays is a slightly conical tube of some twelve feet in length, curled around on itself and opening out into a

How the brass valves work. In the second drawing the column of air, represented by the dotted line, has been deflected by the use of a valve, and thus becomes longer. This lowers the pitch

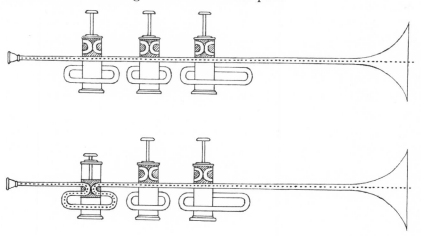

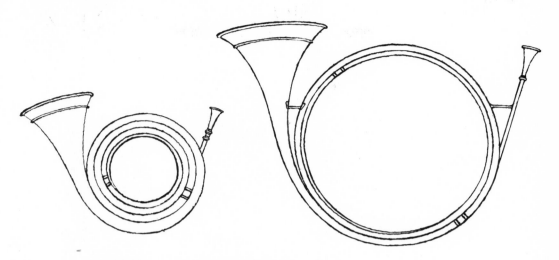

Horns of the seventeenth and eighteenth centuries

very wide bell. The French horn, which was widely used until quite recently, was named F, after its fundamental note. But at the present time most players use a double horn, in which an extra valve puts the instrument into the B flat a fourth higher and allows a greater control of high notes, which on the older French horn were notoriously difficult to pitch accurately. The F horn transposes down a fifth.

The horn has been called "the most romantic of all brass instruments," and certainly it is one of the most versatile, with a large range and a tone that can vary from a peaceful golden splendor to a terrifying blare. In the orchestra the four horns are sometimes a self-contained group, filling the important middle register with warm, sustained harmony; they also blend well with clarinets or bassoons. The first horn player has plenty of solo work too, perhaps especially in the music of German or Austrian composers such as Richard Strauss (1864–1949) and Mahler (1860–1911); but no orchestral composer from Beethoven onward has been indifferent to this beautiful instrument.

The horn

Like all the brass instruments, the horn can be muted. The mute is usually a pear-shaped piece of metal which is fitted into the bell, giving the horn an extraordinary, faraway quality when blown quietly. Another effect is the one called *cuivré*, where the player uses a mute or puts his hand into the bell as far as he can and then blows hard, producing a somewhat strangled but dramatic tone. There are many examples of horn writing which show the instrument in its various moods; Mozart's horn concertos were written for the early instrument without valves and show how much could be done with it, and Britten's *Serenade* and *Nocturne* explore the possibilities of the modern horn thoroughly.

In the orchestra, the first and third horns usually play the higher notes, while the second and fourth play the lower ones. A fifth horn (called a bumper-up) is sometimes seen, even when the music only calls for four; he can take over the first horn part, for example in full orchestral passages, to allow that player a rest before an important solo.

The trumpet is the most military of the brass. A modern trumpet is usually pitched in C or B flat, with a length of four feet or more; like the horn, it is not a straight tube but is bent back on itself, and it has valves—three of them. But unlike the horn, it has a nearly cylindrical bore. The range of a B flat instrument is a tone lower than that of a C trumpet.

The history of the trumpet goes back a very long way, and by the sixteenth century the instrument was recognizable as the one we know today. Bach used it a good deal, for example in his second Brandenburg Concerto. The instrument was without valves in his time, and his trumpet parts lie very high, in the register where the closeness of the harmonics allowed melodies to be written. The addition of valves made the trumpet a fully chroma-

Horn, trumpet, and tenor trombone mouthpieces

The trumpets

tic instrument; but even now, like the other brass, it seems more suited to "plain" writing than to intricate melody. In fact, the quality of its tone, simple and forthright, makes it the ideal instrument for direct musical statement. Yet there is not a very great deal of solo writing for the trumpet in orchestral scores. Of course there are solo *passages* in plenty of works, but nothing to correspond in length and importance to the English horn tune in Sibelius's *The Swan of Tuonela*, the cello solo in the slow movement of Brahms's Second Piano Concerto, or the horn melody in the slow movement of Tchaikovsky's Fifth Symphony. Perhaps this is because really long solos in orchestral music are usually rather slow and expressive; for this, soft playing is needed, and the trumpet is not so well suited to gentle melody. For short, powerful themes on the other hand, it can provide the ideal tone color—as for example the sword motive in Wagner's cycle of music dramas, *The Ring of the Nibelung*.

The practice of muting the trumpet is quite an old one, but it was in fact Wagner (1813–1883) who made this effect really familiar to audiences. The normal mute, conical in shape, is interchangeable with two others, often used in popular music and sometimes asked for by "serious" composers. These are the cup and wa-wa (or wow-wow) mutes. A good example of three trumpets playing together, with ordinary mutes, is at the start of the middle section in Debussy's *Fêtes*, where they sound mysteriously distant.

THE TROMBONE

There are usually three trombones in an orchestra—two tenors and a bass. They are of fairly narrow, cylindrical tubing. There are no valves; instead the player has a U-shaped section of tube at the point where the instrument bends back on itself, which can be pushed outward to a certain extent, so lengthening the air column. There are seven positions of the slide, moving the pitch by a semitone at a time. Thus with the use of harmonics—which are obtained, as with the other brass, by the lips—the player has a fully chromatic range (see p. 89). Many trombone players use a B flat instrument with a thumb valve lowering the pitch to F (a "trigger" trombone) so as to incorporate the range of both the tenor and the bass.

The trombone, with its slide, has a history of at least six hundred years—sackbut is the old English name for it. Unlike the other brass

Cup and wa-wa trumpet mutes

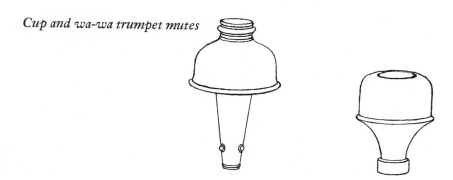

The trombone

instruments, it has always been chromatic—that is, not confined to any particular harmonic series—because of the slide mechanism. There is a magnificent trombone solo in Mozart's *Requiem*, in the "Tuba Mirum" section, which gives some idea of the melodic playing of the instrument. But many people do not feel that lyrical melody suits it; it is too solemn and awe-inspiring, even when played softly. Mozart himself used the tremendous sound of chords on the three trombones in *Don Giovanni*, and so did Beethoven at the height of the storm in the "Pastoral" Symphony.

Trombones, like the other brass, can be muted. They can also

Bass tubas

bear tries a few lumbering dance steps. But unfortunately for the tuba, for many people there is something irresistibly comic about this large and podgy instrument. When one hears it solo, some-how Danny Kaye's record of "Tubby the Tuba" and the late Gerard Hoffnung come to mind. As a matter of fact, the sub-terranean sounds of the bass tuba are not the lowest in the family. There also exist large contrabass tubas, giant sub-bass tubas and even an immense sub-contrabass tuba; but these are curiosities and not orchestral instruments.

48

play what is called *glissando*—sliding from one note to another, just as a string player can slide up or down a string. This can sound very funny, provided it is not done too often. It can also sound rather frightening, as it does in Stravinsky's *Le Sacre du printemps*.

The other member of the brass section is the tuba. Surprisingly enough it belongs to the family of bugles, as it has a wide conical bore. It is often required to provide a foundation for the orchestral brass, though its round, rather blurting tone does not really blend with that of trombones or trumpets. Its length of tubing is about twelve feet, and since it is quite a modern instrument, it has always had valves. The normal orchestral instrument is a bass tuba. In a military band, where the tuba has an important part to play, it is called the bombardon—a splendid name for it—and a smaller version in B flat is called the euphonium. In the orchestra this B flat tuba is called a tenor tuba—Strauss uses one in *Don Quixote*, and there is a long and important solo in Ravel's orchestral version of Mussorgsky's *Pictures at an Exhibition*: it is in the section called "Bydlo [a Polish ox wagon]." The bass tuba features quite prominently in Stravinsky's *Petrouchka*, in the scene where a performing

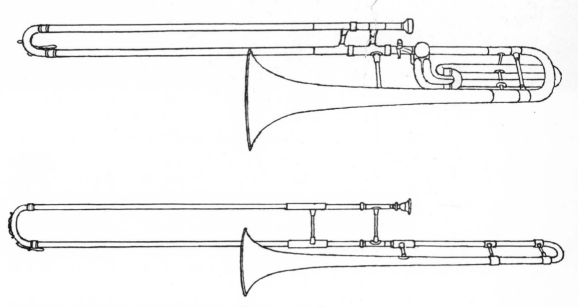

Above: the B Flat/F trombone. Below: the tenor trombone

There are quite a number of brass instruments which have never found a regular place in the orchestra. For example, there are the bugles (the family to which the tuba belongs); small trombones and extra large ones; small trumpets and a "bass trumpet"; and the cornets. The cornet has the same pitch as the trumpet, but is of conical bore—its tone is sweeter but less noble than the trumpet's, and it is somewhat easier to play. French composers quite often use cornets; Debussy does in *La Mer*. The smaller horns should also be mentioned. They are sometimes used in performances of classical works where the horn parts lie uncomfortably high, as they do in some of Haydn's music. The saxhorn family was patented by Adolphe Sax in 1845; these instruments are related to the bugle, and have valves. Mahler's Seventh Symphony opens with a solo for one of them: the tenor saxhorn in B flat.

4

The Percussion

The percussion instruments are all struck in one way or another, and the material struck may be skin, metal, or wood. Some instruments, such as the timpani or xylophone, produce notes; others, like the castanets, give sounds of no definite pitch. This second kind is the more common numerically, and includes all the drums except the timpani.

The percussion section is sometimes called the "kitchen." This affectionate nickname is not such a bad one, for the section has its exotic, spicy sounds as well as clatterings and bangs and splashes; the orchestral *haute cuisine* of those great French chefs, Debussy and Ravel, owes quite a lot to percussion effects which, like strong spices, could not be taken alone but add something to the flavor of the rest. Books on orchestration usually warn students of the danger of too much use of percussion—a quiet roll on a cymbal is probably much more effective than prolonged clashings and crashings. But the use of percussion, as of all orchestral instruments, is governed by one rule only—the composer's instinct for what is right at a particular moment.

THE TIMPANI The timpani, or kettledrums, were the first percussion instruments to win a regular place in the orchestra. Once Hungarian military drums whose origins were Arabian, they have been standard orchestral instruments since the eighteenth century. In the time of Bach and Handel two instruments were used, tuned to the principal notes of a key: tonic and dominant. The octave tuning is thought to have been invented by Beethoven in his last two symphonies. Nowadays three timpani are standard.* They are of dif-

* Large orchestras often have four; this reduces tuning in the course of the music.

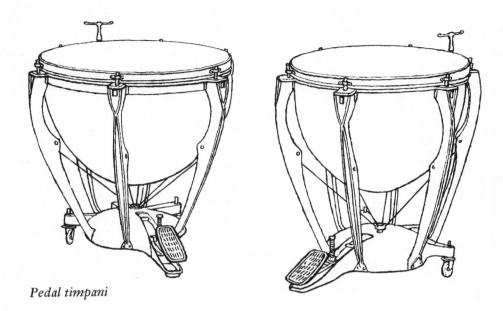

Pedal timpani

ferent sizes; the largest drum, usually to the player's left, gives the lowest notes. In fact, the timpani's range, with three drums, is a comfortable tenth.

Their construction is straightforward: usually the drum is a copper bowl with a calfskin, or often a sheet of plastic, stretched across the top. The pitch of a note depends not only on the diameter of the skin, or head, but also on its tension—the tighter the skin, the higher the note. Each drum can produce six or seven notes—a range of a perfect fourth for the small drum. Most instruments are tuned by screwing a series of taps around the head; some modern ones have in addition a foot pedal to tighten or relax the skin. These pedal timpani have a great advantage of speed and convenience, and the rapid changes of tuning in some twentieth-century works would be impossible without them.

Like all drums, the timpani can play a roll. For this the skin is kept in vibration by the very quick alternation of the two sticks.

51

Played quietly, this sounds like a sustained note. The piano, which is also strictly speaking a percussion instrument, does the same sort of thing in a trill. In fact the same notation is used: the sign *tr* followed by a wavy line. The timpanist has several pairs of drumsticks of different kinds, which he selects according to the nature of the music; the striking end is normally of felt-covered wood. The drums can be muted by placing a cloth over the skin and so reducing vibration; and for the opposite effect, hard wooden sticks can be used. The timpani can be heard to thrilling effect in the Scherzo of Beethoven's Ninth Symphony, where they take on the importance of a solo instrument. Quite a different use of them— but in its way just as exciting—is in the slow movement of Berlioz's *Symphonie fantastique;* here *four* drums are played simultaneously to suggest muffled thunder. A modern work with a virtuoso pedal-timpani part is Britten's *Nocturne* for tenor and chamber orchestra.

The other main percussion instruments are the side drum, bass drum, and cymbals. The side drum, sometimes called the snare drum, is the smallest of the orchestral drums. Like the timpani, it has a military background. It is made of metal or wood, and has a skin at both ends. The depth varies from three to eleven inches, and the diameter is fourteen inches. Outside the lower head, which is not struck, are stretched several gut or wire strings, the snares. When the drum is played, the skin vibrates against these and gives a dry rattling sound. To get a muted effect, the snares can be slackened. The side drum—like all drums except the timpani—has no definite pitch, and its part is all written on one line. The roll is played with a pair of strokes from each hand alternately, and takes a lot of practice to do smoothly. The sticks are of wood, and give a sharper sound than the softer-headed timpani sticks.

THE SIDE DRUM

The tenor drum is more than a useful fill-in for the gap between side and bass drums: it has a somber flavor all its own. It is usually played with soft-headed sticks, and its body is larger in depth and diameter than the side drum's. It is not very common in the orchestra, though Wagner uses it in his opera *Die Walküre*. Brit-

THE TENOR DRUM

53

The timpani

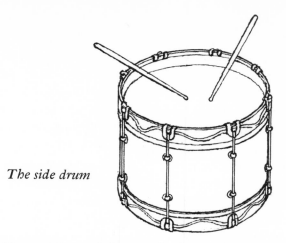

The side drum

ten's opera *The Rape of Lucretia* has a quiet but exciting passage in which only the percussion play: bass drum, tenor drum, side drum with slackened snares and a cymbal. The fact that no instruments of definite pitch are playing creates a problem for anyone who tries to play the music on the piano!

Just now the phrase was used: "the gap between side and bass drums." Although these instruments do not produce definite notes, the general pitch effect corresponds to their size; the side drum quite clearly sounds higher than the tenor drum, and the bass drum is the deepest of the three. In the same way the triangle sounds higher than the middle-pitched cymbals and the deep-voiced gong. This is because the over-all effect of a noise is usually in some general frequency range. Thus a speaking voice can be high or low, though no definite musical notes are produced; or again we can think of the difference between a click and a thud—one high, one low. This is an important matter where percussion is concerned.

THE BASS DRUM   The big bass drum was once called the Turkish drum after the Turkish bands of Mozart's Vienna, which featured it as well as the cymbals, triangle, and sometimes the tambourine. These particular instruments were used by Mozart to provide local color for the Turkish story of his opera *The Seraglio.* Haydn in his "Military" Symphony, and Beethoven in the finale of his Ninth Symphony also used them. The bass drum has two main functions: in soft

54

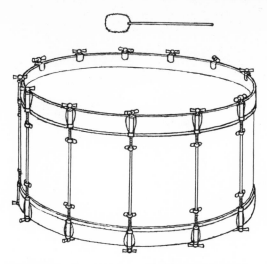

The bass drum

passages to convey a feeling of awe, and in loud ones to add its sheer weight and power to the general proceedings. It has a narrow wooden shell and usually only one skin, unlike the side and tenor drums which have two. A single stick is used, with a heavy felt head; because the instrument is so reverberant, the roll can be played with one stick only.

The tambourine is a small shallow drum with one skin and jingles set into the shell. These are small metal plates hung in pairs, like tiny cymbals, which give a tinkling sound when the instrument is struck or shaken. The three main ways of playing the tambourine are by striking the skin with the hand, shaking the instrument, and running the thumb around the skin—rather a tricky effect which gives the tambourine roll. The instrument is prominently used in the "Arab Dance" in Tchaikovsky's "Nutcracker" Suite.

The triangle is a metal rod bent into a triangular shape, with an open corner. It is hung by a piece of gut or nylon, and struck with a short metal beater. For a roll, this beater is moved back and forth across a corner, inside the instrument as it were. The delicate triangle "ting" is a charming touch of color in soft music; while the Frenchman Widor, in his textbook on orchestration, says that at the climax of an orchestral crescendo "it suffices to add the triangle, in order to convert red-heat into white-heat." Liszt's E flat major Piano Concerto is sometimes called the "Triangle"

THE TAMBOURINE

THE TRIANGLE

55

The tambourine

Concerto, for the instrument has quite an important part. And Brahms, who was not given to exotic effects for their own sake, wrote a number of triangle rolls in the Scherzo of his Fourth Symphony.

THE CYMBALS James Blades, one of the best-known living percussionists and a great authority, says of the cymbals: "those wonderful instruments . . . richly deserve the place they hold in the percussion section of the orchestra." They are two brass plates, slightly curved and with

The cymbals

a domed center; the player holds them by two straps. The cymbal clash is one of the most famous orchestral effects: for this, the metal plates are quickly swept against each other with a glancing blow. A single suspended cymbal can also be struck with a soft or hard stick, and the roll is played with two timpani sticks also on a suspended cymbal. The "sizzle" of the cymbal roll, even in the quietest passage, gives a unique feeling of tension to the music.

The antique cymbals, used by Berlioz, by Debussy in *L'Après-* THE ANTIQUE CYMBALS

57

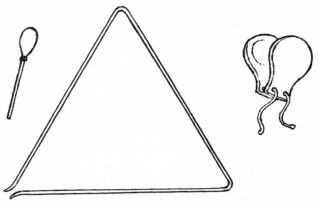

Triangle and beater, and castanets

midi d'un faune, and by Stravinsky, do produce notes of definite pitch—rather high ones. They are two to four inches across and about a quarter of an inch thick—much thicker than the standard, large cymbal. An ancient Hellenistic pair in the British Museum still give out a clear, high F sharp; they bear the Greek inscription "I belong to Oata."

THE GONG The gong comes from the Far East and is an awesome instrument, used sparingly by composers. The large Chinese gong, or tam-tam, may be three or four feet in diameter—a great plate of beaten bronze with a turned-back rim. Until recently the art of successful gong manufacture remained an oriental mystery even in an age of advanced Western technology, but nowadays good instruments are made elsewhere. The crescendo roll on the gong must be heard to be believed: no great strength is needed to produce a volume of sound which could deafen a listener, or the player. In Stravinsky's *Le Sacre du printemps* the very earth seems to quake as the gong player reaches half power or less. A single very soft stroke is awe-inspiring, too; there are examples in Elgar's *Dream of Gerontius* and Tchaikovsky's *Symphonie pathétique*.

THE CASTANETS The castanets are associated with Spain and its neighboring countries, where they are held in the hands of dancers. They are pairs of small wooden clappers, which in orchestral use are often attached to a handle. When the handle is shaken or tapped against the hand, the clappers beat against it, producing their unmistakable sound. Almost all musical evocations of Spain, like Bizet's opera *Carmen*, Debussy's *Ibéria*, and Rimsky-Korsakov's *Capriccio Espagnol*, feature the castanets—a sure way of creating a Mediterranean atmosphere.

The next four instruments belong to the group called tuned percussion—they can play a melody. The glockenspiel, whose name means "play of bells," has usually a range of three full octaves and consists of steel bars, each tuned to a different note; they are arranged like a piano keyboard, with the "black" notes in an upper row. The notes are written two octaves below their actual pitch; this is to avoid the excessive use of ledger lines, for the highest note is the top note of a full-range piano. The glockenspiel is usually played with two beaters with wooden, hard-rubber, or plastic heads. Its clear tone sounds absolutely right in "Mercury" —Holst's exhilarating flight through the upper air in *The Planets*— and it appears in a more down-to-earth setting in the "Dance of the Apprentices" in Wagner's opera *Die Meistersinger*. THE GLOCKENSPIEL

The xylophone is known to most people from Saint-Saëns's *Danse macabre*, where its dry tone suggests the rattle of bones. It is like the glockenspiel except that it has wooden bars with resonators underneath them, a larger range (up to four octaves), and is written for at its proper pitch. Its most effective range is from about A above middle C to a twelfth above. THE XYLOPHONE

The vibraphone appeared in America in about 1920. Its bars are made of a special light alloy which gives a mellow tone, and each bar has a metal tube underneath which acts as a resonator. Inside the top of each tube is a fan which rotates to give a throbbing effect to the sound. The instrument has a pedal, like a piano, to dampen the sounds and prevent them from overlapping. The vibraphone is sometimes played with three or four sticks for chords, as it is in the opening section of Britten's *Spring Symphony*. THE VIBRAPHONE

The tubular bells were brought into the orchestra because composers wanted bell sounds, and the ordinary church bell is far too THE TUBULAR BELLS

59

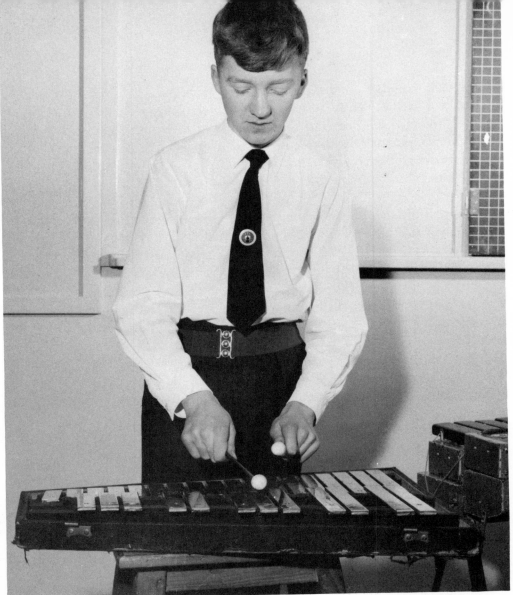

The glockenspiel

large and, since it weighs several tons, far too heavy. The normal orchestral instrument is a set of suspended metal tubes, hung in two rows keyboard-fashion, with an octave range upward from E♭ above middle C; it is fitted with a damping mechanism. The sound of these bells is somehow an exciting one—in Tchaikovsky's *1812 Overture* their effect is overwhelming, while there is a most extraordinary solo in Britten's opera *The Turn of the Screw*, in the church scene.

The celesta is, of course, a percussion instrument, but since it has a keyboard it has been treated in the chapter called "Keyboard Instruments and the Voice."

Among exceptional percussion instruments are the Chinese block, a small partially hollow block of wood, struck with a hard stick; the anvil, used by Wagner in *Das Rheingold* and Walton in *Belshazzar's Feast;* the rattle, which can be heard in Strauss's *Till Eulenspiegel;* the whip, two strips of wood hinged together; small tuned gongs; and the marimba, a form of deep-toned xylophone. Then there is the wind machine—strictly speaking not a percussion instrument, and hardly a wind instrument! This is a cloth-covered cylinder turned by a handle; the cloth is in contact with wooden

A single row of tubular bells

The xylophone

or below; he can also couple one keyboard to another as if he were playing on both at once.

In the Middle Ages a large church organ, such as the one at Winchester in the tenth century, might have as many as ten pipes to each note and two keyboards, or manuals. The Winchester organ apparently required seventy men to provide the wind supply by means of bellows. But most of the organs up to the seventeenth century were small, and even sometimes portable, like an accordion. The pedal board was added in the fourteenth century, and a full control over the various ways of combining stops was reached soon after. By the seventeenth century, organs were built for which Bach wrote—that is, instruments which are in all essentials the same as those we know. Bach's instruments are called baroque organs; some more modern instruments are rather heavier in tone and achieve weight and grandeur at the expense of clarity.

When the organ is used as part of a small-orchestra texture, as in a Bach Cantata, the general preference is for a small baroque-style instrument, or the use of delicate stops on a large one. The difficulty of mixing organ tone into an orchestral texture is a double one: the organ tones tend to cancel out or drown the orchestral ones, and the organ is complete in itself, providing both melody and harmony, so that it is difficult to accompany it. The instrument is usually used very selectively in a Bach performance, coming more to the fore in recitative passages where, with the string bass, it accompanies a voice. On the rare occasions where it is used orchestrally by a nineteenth- or twentieth-century composer, the treatment is often quite different—the sheer power of the instrument is brought in to make a great climax really overwhelming. Holst uses the instrument in this way in *The Planets*. Parts for organ are usually optional, for as a rule only the largest concert halls possess one. Three of Britten's works, written for church performance (and thus not symphonic), use an organ with a small orchestra: *Saint Nicolas*, *Noye's Fludde* and *Curlew River*. His *War Requiem* has an optional "grand organ" part, entering at the biggest climax in the music, and a part for small organ or har-

Baroque organ

monium (a movable organ) which plays almost entirely separate from the orchestra—thus illustrating the two uses of the instrument I have described.

The piano, or pianoforte to give it its full name, was invented by an Italian, Cristofori, about 1709. He called it "a harpsichord with soft and loud." In fact various experiments had been made along piano lines before Cristofori's time, but he was the first to carry his ideas into general musical life, and his instrument, which had a damper action, was much more a true piano than anything earlier. In the modern piano the strings are struck with hammers, which immediately on impact fall away so that the string may go on vibrating; when the key is released, the felt pad called the damper falls against the string and cuts off the sound. A damper foot pedal (the right-hand one) keeps all the dampers away from the string, so that a note may last as long as the string audibly vibrates. The soft pedal, on the left, mutes the sound—on a grand piano this is usually done by shifting the hammers so that only two of the three unison strings provided for each note are struck. For, although we usually speak of a piano string as if it were single, three unison strings are provided for all the upper notes, and two or one for the more resonant lower ones.

Bach pointed out certain defects in the pianos he tried in 1726, but improvements were made, and later on he praised the instrument. One of his sons, Johann Christian, became famous as a pianist as well as a composer. By Mozart's time the instrument had almost completely replaced the harpsichord, and Mozart's piano concertos and sonatas show the fondness he had for the instrument. Incidentally, the damper pedals of Mozart's and even Beethoven's time had less effect of sustaining notes than modern ones—a fact which needs to be borne in mind when playing Beethoven's music in particular.

The piano is sometimes used orchestrally. The fact that it is complete in itself, with melody and harmony, like the organ, makes it difficult for it to take an orchestral place among equals. If a composer's piano part becomes too elaborate and interesting, the

The grand piano

music sounds like a concerto with orchestral accompaniment—all very well of its kind, but here we are speaking of the piano used as *part* of the orchestra, not a solo instrument *with* orchestra. One might almost say that the ideal orchestral use of the piano was such that one would not notice that the instrument was playing! Richard Strauss, Stravinsky, and Shostakovich are among the composers of our time who make occasional orchestral use of the piano. One of the most extraordinary passages in a symphonic movement occurs in Shostakovich's youthful First Symphony: loud staccato chords for solo piano. Surprisingly, it works!

THE CELESTA

The celesta was invented by a Parisian maker, Mustel, and the story is often told of Tchaikovsky coming across the instrument in Paris when it was quite unknown, and later using it in the "Dance of the Sugar-Plum Fairy" in his ballet *The Nutcracker*. The celesta looks like a small piano and has a keyboard and resonators. Its part is written on two staves an octave below pitch, and the range is four octaves upward from middle C. In Richard Strauss's opera *Der Rosenkavalier*, in the scene where the silver rose is presented, its "celestial" tone is of unique beauty.

THE HUMAN VOICE

The human voice is combined with the orchestra in innumerable works, of course, including all operas. Its *orchestral* use is rather different: this means treating it like an instrument, without words; for as soon as words are used the voice is no longer part of the orchestra. One of the finest examples of the orchestral use of voices is in Holst's *The Planets*, at the end of the work, where a women's choir, wordless and unseen, joins in imperceptibly. Gradually the instruments stop playing, and the voices are left alone to fade into silence. Debussy also uses a women's choir in the last of his three "Nocturnes," *Sirènes;* but here they do represent the song of the Sirens, heard across the sea, and because the voices represent something this is a borderline case. Still, they sing no words. Vaughan Williams uses a solo, wordless soprano in two of his symphonies, the "Pastoral" and the "Antartica," where the effect is of space and loneliness.

It is important to stress again that these examples are quite different from Beethoven's use of voices in the Ninth Symphony, and from Mahler's use of a solo soprano in his Fourth Symphony—these are choral or solo *songs*.

6

The Conductor

The conductor is the person in charge of an orchestral performance. In a small group of players like a string quartet, each musician can see and hear the others; but in even a small orchestra this is impossible.

In the fifteenth and sixteenth centuries the members of a choir were kept together by gestures with an arm or stick. In the second half of the seventeenth century a conductor often used a stick to beat time on a desk or the floor. The great composer of Louis XIV's court, Lully, died in 1687 of an infection caused by striking his foot with a long baton—the word *bâton* is the French for a stick. In Bach's time the baton partly disappeared. Performances were directed by the player of the keyboard continuo part, or the first violinist—the "leader" in fact. By the beginning of the nineteenth century, when Beethoven came to maturity, the baton was once again in use. Beethoven conducted the first performance of his First Symphony in 1800. Yet the practice of directing from a keyboard instrument had not by any means died out; in 1829 Mendelssohn conducted his First Symphony, with "a specially made white stick," from the piano. Nowadays the baton is a light stick with a cork or wooden handle, eighteen to twenty-four inches long. In the theater there is sometimes a tiny lighted electric bulb at the tip so that the conductor's beat may be clearly seen by the orchestra and also from the stage.

People are not always clear about the nature of the conductor's task, and it is worth while examining it in some detail. He plays no instrument, but stands facing the players; his responsibility is to direct and control the way the music is played. Of course he cannot stop a player from making a mistake—the player is responsible for the performance of his part, under the conductor's guidance.

But it is the conductor who is solely responsible for such things as speed, balance between different instrumental sounds, and the maintenance of a precise rhythm throughout the whole body of players. He must know the music in great detail, and how he wants it played; and he must be able to communicate his intentions by means of his gestures. In rehearsal, he can explain to the players what he wants from them—and it is essential that he be able to do this clearly—but in performance, gestures are his only means of communication.

The conductor's baton technique is first and foremost a means of indicating the speed of the music and its rhythm. Music proceeds in units of time called bars, and beating time with a stick is a way of showing the beginning of each bar and also the pulses, or beats, within it. The movements of a conductor's arm and stick will usually form a regular, repeated pattern. The descending stroke marks the first beat of a bar, which is accented; the lift of the baton which precedes the downstroke is the weaker upbeat. If there are only two beats in a bar, in a march perhaps, the pattern is a simple down-up movement. In waltz time, where there are three beats in a bar, the pattern becomes down-across-up. Almost all music resolves itself into rhythmic groups of two or three: four in a bar can be thought of as a pair of twos, but with a much less pronounced accent on the first beat of the second pair: this is beaten as down-left-right-up. This is, however, something of a simplification, for an experienced conductor may depart very considerably from his basic baton technique when he is confident of the orchestra's ability to follow him. When he does so, it is to liberate his gestures so that they can convey more expression to the players.

Obviously a conductor should be a natural leader. The orchestra can respect him and play as he wishes only if he has a thorough

Sir Malcolm Sargent at work in rehearsal

command of the performance. At the same time, only a poor conductor fails to give and take occasionally: if a trumpeter, for example, cannot play a high passage really softly, it would be bad psychology on the conductor's part if he did not accept this with a good grace. He will very often ask the advice of the leader or some other player about such things as the best way of bowing a string passage, or where a breath should be taken by a wind player.

Much of the conductor's work is done in rehearsal. One problem of the present-day musical scene is that, because orchestras are expensive to run, rehearsal time is often too short. If the orchestra is doing a well-known work which they have often played, under a conductor with whose stick technique they are familiar, the performance is not likely to go seriously wrong, though it may be rather uninspired. But sometimes a difficult new work gets far too little rehearsal time, and then the music suffers. A good orchestra will get through somehow, but this is hardly enough. And the conductor is often the one who has to negotiate with concert-giving organizations for adequate rehearsal time, so that he and the orchestra may do justice to the music they are playing.

In orchestral performance, matters of interpretation are the conductor's responsibility. This is a much-discussed subject: why do different musicians perform a work in different ways? Most people would say that the ideal performance realized the composer's intentions exactly. But the composer cannot show exactly the way in which every note is to be played or sung. If he writes "Slowing down to the end," how much should the orchestra slow down? "Slightly louder"—but exactly how much? "With great expression" —in what manner? The conductor must answer these questions; and so he needs an understanding of the style of a composer's work, and a sympathy with it. The composer himself, of course, may change his mind, or not have a single "ideal" interpretation in mind when writing a work. Stravinsky conducted a recorded performance of his *Le Sacre du printemps* in 1929; since then he has conducted it many times and made other recordings of it—and none of his performances is *quite* like the others. In any case, when Shakespeare wrote the part of Hamlet, he did not say that the actor must be of a certain height, his voice of a particular quality, and his diction and gestures of a certain kind: room has to be left for differences of individual temperament and physique. There have been a very few cases of a composer admitting that a particular interpretation was better than his original idea. But there is also the well-known story of how Ravel asked Toscanini not to increase the speed at the end of his *Bolero*, this being against his conception of the music. Toscanini ignored the composer's wishes, and when Ravel complained to him afterward he was quite unrepentant, saying that the music would not have succeeded without the *accelerando*. The great conductor was on this occasion wrong, not only, I think, in principle, but also in practice—for the *Bolero* is most successful played at a steady tempo throughout, as the composer intended it to be.

The famous conductor of the Promenade Concerts, Sir Henry Wood, in a book published in 1945 called *About Conducting*, lists the following "points for the would-be conductor":

I   A conductor must have a complete general knowledge of music.

II   The conductor must have more than a slight acquaintance with every instrument of the orchestra, and if possible, some intensive study of a stringed instrument—preferably the violin.

III   The conductor must play the piano well.

IV   The conductor must have an impeccably sensitive ear, as well as rhythmic and interpretative sense.

V   The conductor must be unafraid of the art of gesture.

VI   The conductor must be a perfect sight-reader and sound musician.

VII   The conductor must study the art of singing.

VIII   The conductor must have a good physique, a good temper, and a strong sense of discipline.

Sir Henry explains each of these points at some length, but we can see already that a good conductor needs many qualities—in fact, one who fully satisfied Sir Henry would be something of a superman! We know that infant prodigies of eight years or so have conducted quite acceptable performances. They certainly could not qualify on all the points listed above—but one suspects that they are probably carried by a first-rate orchestra. Sir Henry also says that a conductor should have a good physique—but it is interesting to note that some of the most famous have continued their careers into their eighties; one thinks of Beecham, Toscanini, Monteux, and Klemperer.

Many conductors have been orchestral players, among them Koussevitsky, Monteux, Barbirolli, and Eugene Ormandy. And so we return to the orchestra itself. No conductor, however gifted, can do without a good orchestra: if he is the player, the orchestra is the most exciting, because the most human, of instruments.

7

The Growth of the Orchestra

The word orchestra comes from a Greek word meaning "a dancing place." In ancient times this referred to an open space where dances were performed to an instrumental accompaniment. At the present time the word is used to mean a body of instruments and their players. Fewer than about ten players are usually called a chamber group or ensemble; from ten to twenty-five may be called a chamber orchestra. A full or "standard" orchestra with a large string section—the sort of orchestra needed to play a Debussy work—numbers about seventy players.

Although many instruments are of great antiquity—the cymbals, for example, have remained practically unchanged for about two thousand years—various things stood in the way of the orchestra's development into the standard form which can now be found anywhere in the Western world. Social factors were among the most important: an orchestra is an expensive thing to run, and only the very rich could afford to maintain one. Until the seventeenth century, music, for most people, was confined to the church or found in the open air—country dancing and singing. The first public concert hall was not opened until 1672, in London; before that it would not have been an economic proposition to rely on a paying audience. A century later, even a great musician like Haydn was in the full-time employ of a wealthy nobleman with a private orchestra.

Then there was the problem of the instruments themselves. For instruments to play together, they must be in tune, and there was no standard tuning, as there is now.* Furthermore, certain in-

* A in the treble clef = 440 cycles per second

78

struments, like the woodwinds, have to be made with extremely fine craftsmanship in wood and metal for good tuning. To blend with others, a player must be able to play softly as well as loudly; and many older instruments, like the oboe's ancestor the shawm, were designed for solo work and had no soft tone. And how could a large group of players keep together, since there was no conductor? In any case, composers did not write music for orchestra when such a thing did not exist, and instrumentalists did not band together while there was no music for them to play.

A monarch or rich nobleman might assemble several players, usually of string instruments, who joined in unison melodies and later played in part music—just as a choir is divided into several voices, each with its own melodic strand. In the sixteenth and seventeenth centuries music was often written "for voices or viols" —which, incidentally, shows us that the manner of writing for instruments and voices was often very similar. One of the earliest examples of an orchestra is the group of players who performed at a marriage in France in 1581: "hautboys, flutes, cornetts, trombones, violas da gamba, lutes, harps, flageolet, and ten violins"— but these musicians seem to have played mostly in small groups rather than all together. In Monteverdi's opera orchestra for *Orfeo*, produced at Mantua in 1607, there were violins, viols of three different sizes, flutes of the end-blown type, cornetts (a now obsolete wind instrument, nothing to do with the modern cornet), trumpets, trombones, harp, harpsichords, and three small organs. Some of the wind instruments were so imperfect that they could only play a few notes, but Monteverdi was a highly inventive man who made the most of the resources he had, and his work encouraged other composers to follow his example as well as helping to bring about improvements in standards of playing and instrumental manufacture.

The strings had taken their place as the foundation of the orchestra. Monteverdi's writing for strings is fairly vocal in style, and he hardly ever takes his violins above the range of a soprano voice. However, he did introduce the pizzicato (plucked) effect

79

and was the first to use the tremolo (drawing the bow quickly back and forth across the string) in a dramatic work. But in solo violin writing, by Marini (1597–1665) for example, large leaps, scale and arpeggio passages, and even harmonics are to be found. These advances in string technique were little by little to find their way into orchestral string writing, as composers came to know of them and performers increased in skill. Henry Purcell (1659–1695) was among the leaders of his time in the boldness and color of his instrumental writing.

Alessandro Scarlatti (1659–1725), the founder of the Neapolitan school of opera, used a string group very nearly the same as the present-day one—first and second violins, violas, cellos, and double basses; the basses played the cello part an octave lower. The wind instruments were used to strengthen the firm string foundation. In the time of Bach (1685–1750) the wind was used with greater freedom, particularly by Bach himself. In his Passions and Cantatas a woodwind instrument often has a solo, or obbligato part that accompanies a vocal solo; evidently the standard of playing had much improved. Trumpets and drums were kept in reserve for big climaxes or special occasions, and did not feature regularly in the orchestra. Handel tended to use a larger orchestra than Bach did. He used the wind instruments as a body, in chords, without the strings—in his choral work, *L'Allegro*, he used the double bassoon—and on occasion he employed three or even four trumpets. He seems to have used horns more than Bach, and in the oratorio *Saul* there are parts for three trombones.

Apart from the strings and the harpsichord, the orchestra still had no standard form, as a glance at Bach's six Brandenburg Concertos shows. The present structure of the orchestra was reached, basically, in the time of Haydn and Mozart. The large-scale classical forms of the symphony and concerto had developed gradually from early operatic overtures, which in Italy had a fast-slow-fast pattern, from the concerti grossi of Corelli and Handel, where a small group of instruments was contrasted with a larger one, and of course from the early concertos by men such as Vivaldi and Bach himself. The orchestration of Haydn's "Clock" Symphony, composed in 1794, is: double woodwind (including the fairly new clarinets), two horns, two trumpets, two timpani, and strings, with the cellos and double basses sharing the same part an octave apart. A famous orchestra of the time, which inspired Mozart with its excellence, was at Mannheim. He wrote: "The orchestra is excellent and strong. On either side there are ten or eleven violins, four violas, two oboes, two flutes and two clarinets, two horns, four cellos, four bassoons and four double basses, also trumpets and drums."

Beethoven (1770–1827) brought the trombones into symphonic writing. His powerful music, some of the most dramatic ever written, needed the weight of extra strings. He also introduced the piccolo and double bassoon, and used up to three or four horns. The timpani became almost solo instruments in his music, and the cellos and the double basses were given melodic passages in their upper range.

The Frenchman Hector Berlioz (1803–1869) was one of the great masters of the orchestra. Practically all his music is orchestral, and his book on orchestration is still studied. In his orchestra we find the English horn and tuba, harps and cornets—and the effect of muting not only strings but wind instruments. His *Requiem* calls for at least two hundred voices and an orchestra to match, including sixteen timpani and four brass bands. His "ideal" orchestra, a dream he never realized, had two hundred and forty strings, thirty each of pianos and harps, and the remainder of the orchestra to the same scale of size!

By the middle of the last century, valved horns and trumpets were widely available, and this meant that at last all the blown instruments were fully chromatic, producing any note within their range. Wagner (1813–1883) took full advantage of the improvements in the brass, and with him the brass section was expanded to a great size. In the four music dramas (or operas) called *The Ring of the Nibelung* he employed new instruments called Wagner tubas; actually they are not tubas but are related to the

saxhorns and are played with horn mouthpieces. Wagner also introduced a genuine tuba—a four-valved contrabass. Neither the Wagner tuba nor the contrabass tuba has taken a regular place in the orchestra, though Bruckner and Strauss used the former instrument. Wagner also took advantage of the rapidly improving standards of playing among rank and file orchestral musicians: the very high passage for violins in the Prelude to *Lohengrin* might well have been impossible to orchestral players of fifty years earlier.

By the beginning of this century, the orchestra required by composers such as Richard Strauss and Mahler had grown to proportions which now seem to us excessive. In Strauss's tone poem *Ein Heldenleben* the requirements are: three flutes, piccolo, three oboes, English horn, two clarinets, a small clarinet, a bass clarinet, three bassoons, double bassoon, eight horns, five trumpets, three trombones, tenor tuba, bass tuba, two harps, timpani, side drum, tenor drum, bass drum, cymbals, and a large string section of sixty-six players. A reaction against the use of such enormous forces set in around the time of the First World War—partly because of the altered circumstances due to it, which included a lack of money for huge enterprises. This is symbolized by the difference in requirements between two Stravinsky works: *Le Sacre du printemps*, produced in 1913, uses quadruple woodwind, eight horns, and everything else to match (except that there is no harp part)—but *L'Histoire du soldat* of 1918 calls for seven players only. Later Stravinsky planned another work, *Les Noces*, for large orchestra and then abandoned this idea, finally scoring it for a modest, though unusual ensemble. Stravinsky's mind is always open to new orchestral ideas; he has written music for wind instruments only, as well as for strings alone. Yet one of his more recent works, the *Movements for Piano and Orchestra* of 1959, uses a near-standard orchestra—which, however, has no timpani or horns—and his two symphonies of the nineteen-forties remain within a fairly conventional orchestral framework.

Other modern composers—such as Sibelius, Shostakovich, Walton, Vaughan Williams, Bloch, Hindemith, Copland, Bartók,

83

For the performance of some music the size of the orchestra is considerably augmented

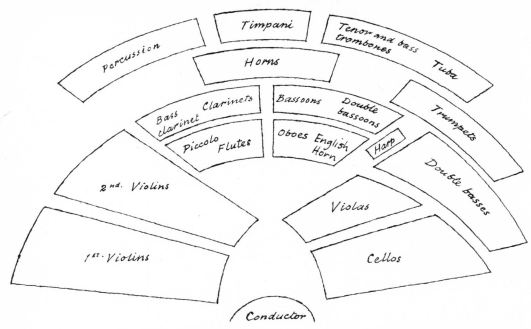

Orchestral seating plans vary, but this arrangement is a common one

Prokofiev, and Britten—have shown themselves satisfied with the symphony orchestra much as Beethoven knew it. The truth seems to be that one can achieve a very wide range of orchestral color with the instruments already available. We should, however, mention one quite new instrument which has made rare orchestral appearances: the ondes Martenot, which was first heard in 1928. The French composer Messiaen (born in 1908) has given it an important part in some of his music. It is an electrophone, in which melody is produced by varying the speed of vibration of electronic valves. To be more precise, what is varied is the relative speed of oscillation of a pair of thermionic valves—something easily understood by a physicist, but not by all musicians!

Nobody knows what the future of the orchestra will be. The first conductor of the Promenade Concerts, Sir Henry Wood, imagined in 1924 an ideal festival orchestra of two hundred players, offering every instrumental resource. Composers of the younger generation, who have become well known since the Second World War, have combined electronic effects (prerecorded on magnetic tape) with the instruments of the normal orchestra. Stockhausen has written a work called *Groups* in which three orchestras with three conductors perform separately and together; a special seating arrangement, if not a special kind of concert hall, is necessary for such music to be heard properly.

But the symphony orchestra as we know it must last while the music of the classical composers is played—that is, from Haydn onward, including most composers of our own time. With its different sections, at times contrasting, at times blending with each other, with its range from the most delicate to the most overwhelming effects, the orchestra has been—and perhaps for some time still will be—the medium through which some of the deepest thoughts of composers are expressed. It has a noble history of nearly two hundred years—and, we hope, a rich future.

ORCHESTRAL EXAMPLES OF
INSTRUMENTAL USE

This list is, of course, nothing like comprehensive. It aims at no more than giving at least one example of each main instrument being prominently featured in an orchestral composition. Concertos are excluded, being in a category of their own. Britten's Variations and Fugue on a Theme of Purcell (*The Young Person's Guide to the Orchestra*) covers all the standard instruments and is recommended listening.

VIOLIN:	*Scheherazade*, Rimsky-Korsakov
	Siegfried (Act III), Wagner
VIOLA:	*Don Quixote*, Richard Strauss
	Enigma Variations (Var. VII), Elgar
CELLO:	Second Piano Concerto (slow movement), Brahms
DOUBLE BASS:	First Symphony (slow movement), Mahler
	A Midsummer Night's Dream (Act III), Britten
HARP:	Symphony in Three Movements (slow movement), Stravinsky
PICCOLO:	Fourth Symphony (Scherzo), Tchaikovsky
FLUTE:	*Prélude à l'après-midi d'un faune*, Debussy
BASS FLUTE:	*Daphnis et Chloé*, Ravel
OBOE:	Eighth Symphony (slow movement), Schubert

ENGLISH HORN:	*The Swan of Tuonela*, Sibelius
OBOE D'AMORE:	Mass in B minor (*Et in Spiritum Sanctum*), Bach
CLARINET:	*Francesca da Rimini*, Tchaikovsky
	First Symphony (opening bars), Sibelius
CLARINET:	*The Nutcracker* ("Dance of the Sugar-Plum Fairy"), Tchaikovsky
BASSOON:	*Le Sacre du printemps* (opening bars), Stravinsky
	The Sorcerer's Apprentice, Dukas
DOUBLE BASSOON:	Piano Concerto for Left Hand (opening bars), Ravel
TRUMPET:	*Petrouchka*, Stravinsky
CORNET:	*La Mer*, Debussy
HORN:	*Till Eulenspiegel* (opening bars), Richard Strauss
	Fifth Symphony (slow movement), Tchaikovsky
TROMBONE:	Sixth Symphony ("Storm"), Beethoven
	Pulcinella, Stravinsky
TUBA:	*Petrouchka*, Stravinsky
	Don Quixote, Richard Strauss
ALTO SAXOPHONE:	*Sinfonia da Requiem*, Britten
	Job, Vaughan Williams
TIMPANI:	Ninth Symphony (Scherzo), Beethoven
	Le Sacre du printemps, Stravinsky
PERCUSSION (general):	Eighth Symphony, ...
	Music for Strings, Percussion and Celesta, Bartók
PIANO:	*Symphony of ...*
ORGAN:	*War Requiem ...*

INSTRUMENTAL RANGE

The following table is a list of the working ranges of the principal instruments dealt with in this book; the term "working range" indicates the full range for normal use but excludes the few extra notes which are available to virtuoso players of certain instruments, as well as high string harmonics and low brass "pedal notes." To avoid an excessive number of ledger lines, the signs 8va————‖ and 8va—————have been used, which mean one octave lower and one octave higher respectively. The ranges of transposing instruments are written at the *actual pitch* of the notes. Only the treble and bass clefs are used; this is for convenience in reading, though certain instrumental parts are normally written in the alto and tenor clefs. The harpsichord, organ, and piano are omitted.

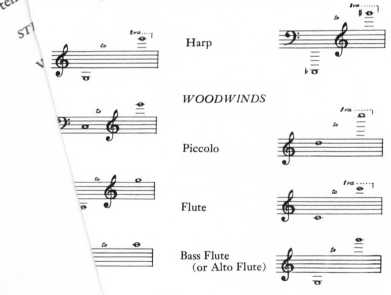

Harp

WOODWINDS

Piccolo

Flute

Bass Flute
(or Alto Flute)

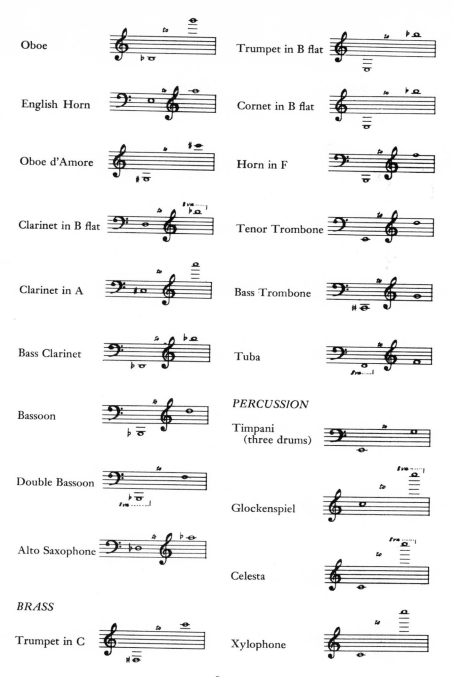

Oboe

English Horn

Oboe d'Amore

Clarinet in B flat

Clarinet in A

Bass Clarinet

Bassoon

Double Bassoon

Alto Saxophone

BRASS

Trumpet in C

Trumpet in B flat

Cornet in B flat

Horn in F

Tenor Trombone

Bass Trombone

Tuba

PERCUSSION

Timpani
(three drums)

Glockenspiel

Celesta

Xylophone

89

SUGGESTIONS FOR FURTHER READING

CARSE, ADAM VON AHN *Musical Wind Instruments*. Macmillan & Company, Ltd., London, 1939

BEKKER, P. *The Story of the Orchestra*. W. W. Norton & Company, Inc., New York, 1936

GEIRINGER, KARL *Musical Instruments*. Oxford University Press, New York, 1945

KENNAN, KENT WHEELER *The Technique of Orchestration*. Prentice-Hall, Inc., New York, 1952

SACHS, CURT *The History of Musical Instruments*. W. W. Norton & Company, Inc., New York, 1940

SCHWARTZ, HARRY WAYNE *The Story of Musical Instruments*. Doubleday, Doran & Company, Inc., New York, 1938

WAGNER, JOSEPH F. *Band Scoring*. McGraw-Hill Book Company, Inc., New York, 1961

Index

antique cymbals, 57–58
anvil, 61

Bach, Johann Christian, 69
Bach, Johann Sebastian, 17, 23, 26, 29, 37, 43, 50, 64, 67, 69, 72, 80–81
Barbirolli, Sir John, 77
Barrère, Georges, 25
Bartók, Béla, 63, 83–84
bass clarinet, 32–34, 35, 83
bass drum, 53, 54–55, 63, 83
bass flute, 35
bass oboe, 35
bassoon, 22, 24–25, 34–35, 81, 83
Beecham, Sir Thomas, 77
Beethoven, Ludwig van, 17, 21, 22, 35, 41, 46, 50, 53, 54, 69, 71, 72, 81, 83–84
Berlioz, Hector, 14, 38, 53, 57–58, 81
Bizet, Georges, 59
Blades, James, 56
Bloch, Ernest, 83–84
Boehm, Theobald, 25
bow, 11, 13–14
Brahms, Johannes, 35, 44, 56
brass instruments (*general*), 39–40. *For individual instruments, see separate subject entries*
Britten, Benjamin, 14, 20, 28, 35, 43, 53, 59, 67–69, 83–84
Bruckner, Anton, 83
bugle, 47, 49

castanets, 50, 58–59

celesta, 61, 71
cello, 9, 11, 12, 14, 16–17, 44, 80, 81
chalumeau, 29
Chinese block, 61
clarinet, 22, 24, 29–32, 81, 83
conductor, 72–77
continuo parts, 16, 64, 72
Copland, Aaron, 83–84
Corelli, Arcangelo, 14, 80
cornet, 49, 79, 81
cornett, 79
Cristofori, Bartolomeo, 69
crooks, 40
cymbals, 50, 54, 56–58, 63, 78, 83

Debussy, Claude, 26, 45, 49, 50, 57–58, 59, 71, 78
Denner, Johann Christopher, 29
double bass, 9, 11, 12, 17–19, 80–81
double bassoon, 22, 35, 80, 81, 83
Dragonetti, Domenico, 17
Dukas, Paul, 35
Dvorak, Anton, 29

electronic music, 84–85
Elgar, Sir Edward, 58
English horn, 29, 32, 37, 44, 81, 83
Érard, Sébastien, 19–20
euphonium, 47

flageolet, 79
flute, 22, 25–26, 79, 81, 83

93

Forsyth, Cecil, 29 (note)
Franck, César, 9

Gabrieli, Domenico, 16
glockenspiel, 59, 63
gong, 54, 58
Goossens, Leon, 29

Handel, George Frideric, 21, 29, 50, 64, 80
harmonium, 67–69
harp, 9, 19–21, 79, 81, 83
harpsichord, 64–65, 79
hautboy, 79
Haydn, Joseph, 17, 29, 49, 54, 64, 78, 81, 85
Heckel, Wilhelm, 35
heckelphone, 35–36
Henry Wood Promenade Concerts, 76–77, 84–85
Hindemith, Paul, 14–15, 83–84
Hoffnung, Gerard, 48
Holst, Gustav, 35, 59, 67, 71
horn, 39, 40–43, 44, 49, 80, 81, 83

Kaye, Danny, 48
keyboard instruments (*general*), 64–71, 72. *For individual instruments, see separate subject entries*
Klemperer, Otto, 77
Koussevitsky, Serge, 77

Liszt, Franz, 55–56
Louis XIV, King of France, 72
Lully, Jean-Baptiste, 72
lute, 79

Mahler, Gustav, 17, 21, 41, 49, 71, 83
mandolin, 21
Mannheim orchestra, 31, 81
marimba, 61
Marini, Biagio, 80
Mendelssohn, Felix, 72
Messiaen, Olivier, 84

Monteux, Pierre, 77
Monteverdi, Claudio, 14, 79
Mozart, Wolfgang Amadeus, 9, 14, 21, 29, 31–32, 43, 46, 54, 64, 69, 80
Mussorgsky, Modest, 47
Mustel, Victor, 71

oboe, 22, 24–25, 28–29, 30, 32, 35–37, 79, 81, 83
oboe d'amore, 37
ondes Martenot, 84
organ, 64, 65–69, 79
Ormandy, Eugene, 77

Paganini, Niccolò, 14
percussion instruments (*general*), 50, 53–55, 61–63. *For individual instruments, see separate subject entries*
piano, 53, 54, 69–71, 72, 76, 81
piccolo, 22, 27–28, 81, 83
Primrose, William, 14
Prokofiev, Serge, 84
Purcell, Henry, 80

rattle, 61
Ravel, Maurice, 20, 26, 35, 38, 47, 50, 76
reeds, 23, 25
Rimsky-Korsakov, Nicolas, 59

Saint-Saëns, Camille, 17, 59
Sax, Adolphe, 32, 38, 49
saxhorn, 49, 81–83
saxophone, 32, 37–38
Scarlatti, Alessandro, 80
Schönberg, Arnold, 21
Shakespeare, William, 76
shawm, 28, 79
Shostakovich, Dmitri, 70, 83–84
Sibelius, Jean, 29, 44, 83–84
side drum, 53, 63, 83–84
Stadler, Anton, 32
Stockhausen, Karl-Heinz, 85
Stradivari, Antonio, 13, 14
Strauss, Richard, 35–37, 41, 47, 61, 70, 71, 83

Stravinsky, Igor, 20, 21, 33–34, 35, 47, 58, 70, 75–76, 83–84

string instruments (*general*), 9–13, 80, 81, 83. *For individual instruments, see separate subject entries*

tambourine, 55

Tchaikovsky, Peter Ilich, 33, 35, 44, 55, 58, 61, 71

tenor drum, 53–54, 83

tenor tuba, 47, 83

timpani, 50–53, 80–81, 83

Toscanini, Arturo, 76, 77

triangle, 54, 63

trombone, 39, 40, 45–47, 49, 79, 80, 81, 83

trumpet, 39, 43–45, 49, 75, 79, 80, 81, 83

tuba, 28, 39, 47–48, 81–83

tubular bells, 59–61

tuned gongs, 61

valves, 40, 43, 47, 49, 81–83

Vaughan Williams, Ralph, 38, 63, 71, 83–84

vibraphone, 59, 63

viol, 17, 79

viola, 9, 11, 14–15, 80–81

viola da gamba, 79

violin, 9–11, 12, 13–14, 76, 79, 80, 81

Vivaldi, Antonio, 16–17, 21, 80

voice, 71, 79, 81

Wagner, Richard, 45, 53, 59, 61, 81–83

Wagner tubas, 81

Walton, Sir William, 14–15, 61, 83–84

whip, 61

Widor, Charles Marie, 55

Winchester organ, 67

wind machine, 61–63

Wood, Sir Henry, 76–77, 84

woodwind instruments (*general*), 22–25, 80, 83. *For individual instruments, see separate subject entries*

ABOUT THE AUTHOR

CHRISTOPHER HEADINGTON is a distinguished composer and pianist who has lectured and written widely on musical subjects. Formerly in the Music Department at Lancing College in England, he was for a time on the staff of the BBC, and is now a lecturer and tutor at Oxford University in England. A graduate of the Royal Academy of Music and now an elected Associate of the Academy, Mr. Headington is also a member of the Composers' Guild of Great Britain, the Incorporated Society of Musicians, and the Performing Right Society. His book, *The Orchestra and Its Instruments*, was runner-up for the Carnegie Medal for the best children's book of the year in England.

1   2   3   4   5   71   70   69   68   67

ENGLISH HORN:	*The Swan of Tuonela*, Sibelius
OBOE D'AMORE:	Mass in B minor (*Et in Spiritum Sanctum*), Bach
CLARINET:	*Francesca da Rimini*, Tchaikovsky
	First Symphony (opening bars), Sibelius
BASS CLARINET:	*The Nutcracker* ("Dance of the Sugar-Plum Fairy"), Tchaikovsky
BASSOON:	*Le Sacre du printemps* (opening bars), Stravinsky
	The Sorcerer's Apprentice, Dukas
DOUBLE BASSOON:	Piano Concerto for Left Hand (opening bars), Ravel
TRUMPET:	*Petrouchka*, Stravinsky
CORNET:	*La Mer*, Debussy
HORN:	*Till Eulenspiegel* (opening bars), Richard Strauss
	Fifth Symphony (slow movement), Tchaikovsky
TROMBONE:	Sixth Symphony ("Storm"), Beethoven
	Pulcinella, Stravinsky
TUBA:	*Petrouchka*, Stravinsky
	Don Quixote, Richard Strauss
ALTO SAXOPHONE:	*Sinfonia da Requiem*, Britten
	Job, Vaughan Williams
TIMPANI:	Ninth Symphony (Scherzo), Beethoven
	Le Sacre du printemps, Stravinsky
PERCUSSION (general):	Eighth Symphony, Vaughan Williams
	Music for Strings, Percussion and Celesta, Bartók
PIANO:	*Symphony of Psalms*, Stravinsky
ORGAN:	*War Requiem*, Britten

INSTRUMENTAL RANGES

The following table is a list of the working ranges of the principal instruments dealt with in this book; the term "working range" indicates the full range for normal use but excludes the few extra notes which are available to virtuoso players of certain instruments, as well as high string harmonics and low brass "pedal notes." To avoid an excessive number of ledger lines, the signs 8va————— and 8va—————have been used, which mean one octave lower and one octave higher respectively. The ranges of transposing instruments are written at the *actual pitch* of the notes. Only the treble and bass clefs are used; this is for convenience in reading, though certain instrumental parts are normally written in the alto and tenor clefs. The harpsichord, organ, and piano are omitted.